SPOTLIGHT ON THE RISE AND FALL OF ANCIENT CIVILIZATIONS™

ANCIENT MESOPOTAMIAN RELIGION AND BELIEFS

LAURA LORIA

ROSEN PUBLISHING

Published in 2017 by The Rosen Publishing Group, Inc.
29 East 21st Street, New York, NY 10010

First Edition

Library of Congress Cataloging-in-Publication Data

Names: Loria, Laura, author.
Title: Ancient Mesopotamian religion and beliefs / Laura Loria.
Description: First Edition. | New York : Rosen Publishing, 2017. | Series: Spotlight on the rise and fall of ancient civilizations | Includes bibliographical references and index.
Identifiers: LCCN 2016003665| ISBN 9781477789155 (library bound) | ISBN 9781477789131 (pbk.) | ISBN 9781477789148 (6-pack)
Subjects: LCSH: Assyro-Babylonian religion.
Classification: LCC BL1620 .L67 2016 | DDC 299/.21—dc23
LC record available at http://lccn.loc.gov/2016003665

Manufactured in the United States of America

CONTENTS

GODS AND GODDESSES

Mesopotamians, the people who settled in the land between the Tigris and Euphrates rivers in modern-day Iraq, Syria, and Turkey, were the first people to live what we today consider civilized lives. They were the first people to introduce systems of agriculture, government, cities, and written language. Even with these advancements, they lived in unpredictable times. Their scientific thought was quite basic, so they relied on their religious beliefs to explain the world around them.

Mesopotamians were polytheistic, which means that they believed in a number of gods and goddesses. This was common with other ancient cultures, too, such as the Greeks and Romans. Myths about these gods and goddesses were used to explain the origin of the earth and natural phenomena. Cults and tribes were usually devoted to individual gods and goddesses, and the deities were thought to protect their cities.

Ancient people felt close to their gods and depicted images of themselves on their temples, as seen on this relief from an Assyrian temple in present-day Iraq.

AN, GOD OF THE UNIVERSE

The god An was the first ruling god of all of the deities of ancient Mesopotamia. His name means "heaven" in Sumerian, and he was thought to live in the highest level of heaven.

An was considered the creator of the universe by the Sumerian and Babylonian people in Mesopotamia. Some stories say he created it alone, while others say he shared the job with his descendants. As creator, he was also supreme ruler. As the god of justice, his decisions were unchangeable.

An could be considered a manager of sorts. He gave powers to lesser gods and ranked them at his will. Although he rarely interfered in human lives, he was called upon to crown kings.

Over time, other rulers came to power, so An's powers changed. His powers were delegated to other gods, and while he was still revered, he was not as important as he had been in the past.

This rendering of the Anu-Adad temple in Assur was the dominant structure in the area, indicating the supreme importance of worship in ancient Mesopotamian culture.

ENLIL, RULER OF THE EARTH

The firstborn son of An, Enlil was said to have created and ruled over the earth. He was worshipped throughout ancient Mesopotamia, particularly in the southern city of Nippur.

He was feared because he both created and destroyed at his will. He could not be convinced to change his mind, so the people praised him highly to stay in his favor. He held the Tablet of Destinies, which was thought to be a slab of clay engraved with the universe's laws. Whichever god held the tablet was omnipotent, or all powerful.

He was described in poems and prayer texts as king and father of the gods, which seems unusual, as his father, An, is said to be the same. While some gods were more significant than others, they did not have an official ranking system. The most powerful god was whichever god the people revered the most, and that changed over time.

This image of Enlil was taken from a cylinder seal, used to create an impression stamped on clay for sealing official documents. It served as a person's signature.

ENKI, GOD OF WATERS

Enki, another son of An, was among the top gods and goddesses in ancient Mesopotamia. He was said to live in a place in the ocean, called the *abzu*, underground. A kinder, more generous god than his brother Enlil, Enki had many roles. Along with water, he was known as the god of magic, wisdom, and craftspeople.

Enki was a life-giver. He had numerous children with several goddesses. While his brother tried to destroy humanity, Enki repeatedly interfered to save it. He is credited with bringing fresh water to the land, making agriculture possible. His magical powers included granting human priests the ability to exorcise demons, which were thought to cause illness.

At some point, Enki also became known as Ea. In art, he is shown with a beard, wearing a helmet and robes, often with fish and moving water. Like his brother, his temple was also located in southern Mesopotamia, in the city of Eridu.

The birds flying through the water coming from Enki's shoulders represent his positive, life-affirming qualities. Other symbols associated with Enki include rams, human-fish, and goat-fish.

MARDUK, GOD OF BABYLON

The main ruling groups of ancient Mesopotamia were the Sumerians, Babylonians, and Assyrians, in that order. When a new group gained power, it would incorporate the gods and goddesses of the former powers while giving higher ranking to its own deities. This is what happened for Marduk, a god who, in Babylonian times, replaced An, Enlil, and Enki as the supreme god.

Marduk was the god of the city of Babylon. His rise in popularity came during the reign of King Hammurabi. After the Assyrians rose to power, they continued to revere him. He was chiefly worshipped in the northern and central parts of Mesopotamia.

Marduk lived on top of a temple called Etemananki in the city of Babylon and was said to come to the city every year to bring blessings to the people. He is depicted as a creature that was known as a *mušḫuššu*, or snake-dragon.

Ancient Mesopotamians performed a variety of rituals to the statues of their gods. They believed that gods, such as Marduk, resided within the statues themselves.

LESSER GODS AND GODDESSES

Like the Greeks and Romans, ancient Mesopotamians had divine beings associated with many aspects of nature and life in general. They were prayed to, written about, and given sacrifices by people. These actions were taken to ask for favors or to prevent anger from the gods. Each city had its own patron god or goddess, and a temple was built for him or her. Over time, many of the gods' and goddesses' names changed, as their myths were spread across Mesopotamia.

Utu was the god of the sun. Also called Šamaš, he was thought to rise every morning and follow the sun's path, watching over people's actions while bringing the light needed to grow crops and warm the earth. He was associated with justice, truth, and protection against curses.

Utu was the son of Nanna, god of the moon, also called Suen. Nanna's temple was in Ur. The Sumerians considered him to be just below An, Enlil, and Enki. Like his son, Nanna was associated with truth and justice, but also with fertility, cows and divination, or prediction of the future.

Even powerful kings were reverent to their gods. King Hammurabi and Utu, shown here, are both important figures in matters of law in ancient Mesopotamia.

The goddess Gula, or Ninkarrak, was known for her healing abilities. One of the daughters of An, she was thought to protect the health of people and the land. Her name was chanted in prayers for the sick. In artwork, she is typically shown seated with a dog at her feet. Three of her descendants were also associated with healing.

Inana was a goddess with a double nature. She was both goddess of love and war, two forces at odds with one another. Although female, Inana, also called Ištar, has both feminine and masculine characteristics. Her parentage is debated, as are her romantic relationships. She had temples in many cities, which highlights her relatively high status among the deities.

Depictions of gods and goddesses, like Gula, typically featured objects found in the natural world, such as stars, the moon, and the sun, and animals.

TEMPLES

Gods and goddesses had homes on earth called temples. Early temples were simple structures made of clay, raised on platforms to protect them from floods. They had either one large room or one large room with a few smaller rooms attached. Within the temple, a raised platform held a throne for the god or goddess, covered by a curtain to protect it from wicked people. Small figures stood on nearby benches, to represent the people of the city who were in need of help from the gods and goddesses.

As building techniques became more sophisticated, so did the temples. They were frequently rebuilt, because the clay broke down over time, and thus improved. Their shapes became more complex. They resembled pyramids, with steps leading up to a tower. The shrine to the god or goddess of the city was at the top, where a statue of the deity could reside and guard over the city and its inhabitants. This was called a ziggurat.

Great care was taken in designing and constructing a ziggurat. This temple in Iraq has stood for nearly four thousand years.

A temple was not only a place to worship. It also served as a city center, for trade and government activities. The temple was where much of the activity of city life took place. Workshops were located near the temple, to provide items for worship. Food was stored there, to feed the temple workers, to provide offerings to the gods, and to hand out to the residents of the city. Merchants would offer their items for sale in and around the temple, as there was plenty of traffic.

Some people worked and lived at the temple, including a group of priests, who ran the temple and all of its activities, and priestesses, whose chief job was to pray. The temple workers also provided for the community, taking in orphans and giving loans to people.

The multileveled structure of ziggurats allowed room for a variety of activities that met the physical and spiritual needs of the community.

PRIESTS

In ancient Mesopotamia, priests were responsible for running the temple, the center of activity for the city. Their duties were primarily religious, but they had to tend to the gods, royalty, and common people.

Their most important duty was to please the gods. Most modern people believe that their higher power is heavenly and has no worldly needs. Mesopotamian gods were regarded as humanlike and subject to the whims of their emotions. If a god was angry, he could bring devastation to a temple community. Therefore, Mesopotamians treated their gods like honored guests, to keep them content. They were routinely bathed, entertained, and "fed" large banquets twice a day, which were then distributed to workers and their families.

Priests had other duties as well. Beyond conducting ceremonies, they kept calendars and star charts, wrote religious texts, kept records, healed the sick, and educated new priests in their traditions. Priests were also businessmen, controlling trade, agriculture, and construction projects.

A depiction of a priest tending to objects associated with the goddess Ištar and the god Sin. Priests took care of their gods as if they were living beings.

RITUALS

Beyond the daily worship at the temple, Mesopotamians held many feasts and celebrations throughout the year. On these occasions, all of the people in the city could join in worship of their gods and goddesses. The celebrations featured parades, songs, and dramatic readings or plays.

One of the most significant festivals was the New Year's festival. It took place over twelve days in the springtime in Babylon. Its highlight was the parade of the statue of Marduk, followed by other statues of "visiting" gods. People would chant verses of the *Enuma Elish* as he passed.

The festival also served to affirm the king's reign. The king would arrive at the temple to be slapped by the high priest. This showed that even kings were lesser than gods. He would enter the temple to pray and would be slapped again on his way out. This showed the people that the gods had approved him for another year of kingship.

Sacrifices of animals were made to appease the gods and goddesses. Artists captured these ceremonies in stone, to decorate the temples.

KINGS AND GODS

In ancient Mesopotamia, kings were regarded as humans with special abilities. They were chosen by the gods to carry out their commands for the ordinary people. This was an awesome responsibility, and the kings took it very seriously.

Early Sumerian kings were also high priests. Therefore, it was their responsibility to ensure that a temple was built to honor the gods. A king would often place the first brick when a temple was constructed, writing his name on it to guarantee that the gods knew who was responsible for its construction.

Kings were responsible for protecting their people from enemies. They built walls around their cities to keep invaders out. They personally led troops into battle, representing their god or goddess to provide protection and bestow blessings upon their warriors. Victories ensured the gods would be pleased with them and earned money and slaves for the kingdom.

Surviving artwork, like this statue of a Sumerian king, show the importance of kings, and give historians knowledge about their dress and appearance.

SACRED WORDS

The Sumerians are credited with inventing cuneiform sometime around 3000 BCE. Cuneiform is the first known system of writing, done on clay tablets. The survival of these tablets is how we have learned about ancient Mesopotamian life, especially about their religious beliefs. By reading their hymns, prayers, and myths, historians have discovered how these people worshipped their gods.

Lists of gods and goddesses were kept in libraries, along with written copies of myths and prayers, to be taught in schools. One such hymn, the "Agushya," tells the story of Ea, or Enki, who began a festival devoted to the goddess Ištar, which calls for people to dance in her honor.

Prayers were recorded asking the gods for help. One prayer to An asks for him to bless a king, first by praising An's best qualities and then asking that they be granted to the king. Simpler prayers from common people were often requests to end suffering and provide food.

A sculpture of the head of the goddess Ištar may have been displayed not only for worship but to educate religious students about their deities.

EPIC OF GILGAMESH

Many cultures have stories that teach an important lesson or highlight a common value of the time. In ancient Mesopotamia, one of those stories was the *Epic of Gilgamesh*. It was first written down around 2000 BCE, but it was undoubtedly a tale passed down orally for many years before that. It is considered one of the first great works of literature.

Gilgamesh was an unpopular king of Uruk. He was brave and strong but also cruel and thoughtless. The wise men of Uruk asked their goddess, Aruru, to teach him a lesson. She sent him a companion named Enkidu, who was physically equal to him but uncivilized. As Enkidu learned to become a good man, Gilgamesh learned how to become a better person himself.

The pair went on many adventures together, seeking immortality, but they failed. Enkidu died at the hands of Ištar. Gilgamesh was humbled to learn that humans cannot be like gods.

The statue of King Gilgamesh of Uruk is considerably larger than the figures surrounding it, indicating his significance. His story was widely known among ancient Mesopotamians.

OMENS AND ASTROLOGY

Ancient people did not have the benefit of science to explain the natural world. When misfortune fell upon them, perhaps in the form of bad weather or illness, they wanted answers. They longed for an explanation and perhaps a way to prevent such disasters from happening in the future.

Omens were signs that foretold future events, the actions of the gods. For some priests, their chief duty was seeking out and interpreting omens and recording them for future reference. Once the information was interpreted, they could advise the king about actions to take. One common method of interpreting an omen was to kill a sheep and dissect its liver. The priests claimed its shape, color, or other features could indicate future events. This was considered a science in ancient times. Labeled clay models of sheep's livers, probably for teaching and reference, have been found in the region.

The writing on the model of an animal's liver, made of terra cotta, describes methods for interpreting an omen from its shape, color, or other features.

Because gods and goddesses were believed to live in the sky, it was logical for the ancient Mesopotamians to look to the stars and planets for clues about their fate. Astronomy, the scientific study of celestial bodies, and astrology, the interpretation of the meaning of their positions, were of equal importance to ancient Mesopotamians.

Astronomers recorded the movements of objects in the sky with surprising accuracy, given their limited tools. They looked through hollowed tubes to isolate celestial bodies and used sundials to record the movement of the sun. They worked in shifts of approximately four hours and recorded their observations on clay tablets. Eventually, they were able to predict future movements, based on patterns that they observed.

Astrologers took that information and assigned meaning to it. The sun, moon, stars, and planets were assigned to gods and goddesses. They interpreted heavenly events to predict earthly events, like wars, deaths, births, and crop outcomes.

The movements of celestial objects were monitored and recorded in order to obtain a better understanding of the natural world.

HEALING

Like other unpleasant aspects of ancient life, illness and disease were thought to be caused by angry gods or demonic spirits. When a person was suffering from a physical problem, he or she consulted a spiritual adviser, called an *ashipu*. The ashipu would examine a sick person and then consult texts, compiled by earlier ashipus, to determine which deity was causing the problem and what the recommended method of treatment was.

First, the ashipu would determine if the patient had done something wrong to deserve the punishment of illness. The patient could pray or make offerings to the god he or she offended, in an attempt to win mercy, or to Damu and Gula, the god and goddess of healing. Spells or incantations might be said over the patient, to drive away a demon or ask for a god's help in doing so. Magic potions were sometimes used as well.

A sacrifice to the gods, such as an animal, was considered necessary to protect oneself from harm. Multiple animals were offered for more serious situations.

BURIAL

In a time when medicine was primitive, death was an ordinary fact of life. The dead were buried underground, as the ancient Mesopotamians believed that the afterlife was there. Underground burial was supposed to make the journey to the afterworld easier for the spirit. Cremation was rare because of the expense of the wood required for burning. The ancient Mesopotamians also believed that the rising smoke would send the spirit to the sky, where only gods lived.

Common people were buried near their homes so that their families could tend their graves. The body might be placed in a large clay jar or laid out wrapped in cloth or in a box. After death, people would be placed with their favorite things, as well as useful items, like food and tools, to make the afterlife more comfortable. The rich and powerful were more likely to have large tombs, with more lavish items, and be buried near the temple or palace.

Elaborate decorations, like this goat's head lyre made from precious metals and stones, were placed on the graves of important people—in this case, a queen.

THE LEGACY OF ANCIENT MESOPOTAMIA

Ancient Mesopotamia is called the Cradle of Civilization for good reasons. Nearly all aspects of civilized society were born there. Perhaps most significant, written records were kept, guaranteeing that the ideas, knowledge, and beliefs of the Mesopotamians would live on.

It is not a coincidence that later religions can trace their practices and beliefs to ancient Mesopotamia. Ideas spread outward from the region and were adapted to fit the cultures that adopted them. For example, the ancient Greek and Roman casts of gods and goddesses were very similar to those of ancient Mesopotamia.

Modern people may regard the Sumerians, Babylonians, and Assyrians as superstitious and silly for their beliefs, but they should not be dismissed. They used their observational skills to attempt to understand the world. They kept records and built upon prior knowledge to develop vast libraries of information. They are the foundation upon which modern life was built.

Museums around the world display ancient Mesopotamian artifacts, such as this seven-thousand-year-old carving of a winged god, for modern scholars to study.

GLOSSARY

ashipu The person who provides healing magic.

celestial Having to do with or placed in the sky or outer space.

cuneiform The ancient Sumerian writing system, which used symbols.

deity A supreme being; a god or goddess

demonic Having to do with demons; evil.

descendant A person whose ancestry can be traced back to another.

divine Having to do with a god or goddess; heavenly.

exorcise To remove evil spirits through rituals.

immortality The ability to live forever.

incantation A series of words used in magic.

omen A sign of events to come.

omnipotent Having complete or limitless power.

orally Spoken rather than written.

polytheistic Belief in more than one god.

primitive Having to do with the early stages of development; uncultured or basic.

revere To show great honor or respect for.

sacrifice An offering to the gods, such as food or a slaughtered animal.

ziggurat A tall structure made for worship.

FOR MORE INFORMATION

The British Museum
Great Russel Street
London WC1B 3DG
England
Website: http://www.thebritishmuseum.ac.uk
The British Museum's website offers access to images of nearly three hundred artifacts from ancient Mesopotamia.

The Metropolitan Museum of Art
1000 Fifth Avenue
New York, NY 10028
(212) 535-7710
Website: http://www.metmuseum.org
Visitors have online access to many ancient Mesopotamian sources.

The Oriental Institute
1155 E. 58th Street
Chicago, IL 60637
(773) 702-9514
Website: http://oi.uchicago.edu
The institute maintains a museum and funds research in Asia and the US.

WEBSITES

Because of the changing nature of Internet links, Rosen Publishing has developed an online list of websites related to the subject of this book. This site is updated regularly. Please use this link to access the list:

http://www.rosenlinks.com/SRFAC/mreli

FOR FURTHER READING

Dalal, Anita, ed. *Ancient Mesopotamia*. London, England: Brown Bear Books, 2009.

Doeden, Matt. *Tools and Treasures of Ancient Mesopotamia*. Minneapolis, MN: Lerner Classroom, 2014.

Feinstein, Stephen. *Discover Ancient Mesopotamia*. New York, NY: Enslow Publishers, 2014.

Head, Tom. *Ancient Mesopotamia*. Edina, MN: Essential Library, 2015.

Hollar, Sherman. *Mesopotamia*. New York, NY: Britannica Educational Publishing, 2012. Ebook.

Lassieur, Allison. *Ancient Mesopotamia*. Chicago, IL: Children's Press, 2012.

Kupier, Kathleen, ed. *Mesopotamia: The World's Earliest Civilization*. Chicago, IL: Britannica Educational Publishing, 2011. Ebook.

Nardo, Don. *Life in Ancient Mesopotamia*. San Diego, CA: Referencepoint Press, 2013.

Nardo, Don. *Mesopotamia*. Mankato, MN: Compass Point Books, 2012.

Wood, Alix. *Uncovering the Culture of Ancient Mesopotamia*. New York, NY: PowerKids Press, 2016.

BIBLIOGRAPHY

Ancient History Encyclopedia. "Burial," "Enheduanna," "Enuma Elish – The Babylonian Epic of Creation," "Gilgamesh," "Mesopotamia," "Mesopotamian Religion," "The Myth of Adapa," "Nebuchadnezzar II," "Temple." March 10, 2014. Retrieved April 2016 (http://www.ancient.eu).

Bancroft-Hunt, Norman. *Living in Ancient Mesopotamia*. New York, NY: Chelsea House, 2009.

Bhugra, Ankita, Anu Meha, Thulasi Raj. "Ancient Mesopotamian Priests." 2013. Retrieved April 2016 (http://www.ancientmesopotamians.com/ancient-mesopotamian-priests.html).

British Museum. "Festivals." Retrieved April 2016 (http://www.mesopotamia.co.uk/staff/resources/background/bg04/home.html).

Choksi, M. "Ancient Mesopotamian Beliefs in the Afterlife." June 20, 2014. Retrieved April 2016 (http://www.ancient.eu/article/701/).

Grand Valley State University. "The Story of Atrahsis." 2005. Retrieved April 2016 (http://faculty.gvsu.edu/websterm/atrahasi.htm).

HistoryCentral. "World History." 2015. Retrieved April 2016 (http://www.historycentral.com/dates/).

Jacobsen, Thorkild. "Mesopotamian Religions: An Overview [First Edition]." *Encyclopedia of Religion*. Lindsay Jones, ed. 2nd ed. Vol. 9. Detroit: Macmillan, 2005. *World History in Context*. November 17, 2015.

Nardo, Don. *Ancient Mesopotamia*. Farmington Hills, MI: Lucent, 2004.

"Omens in the Ancient World." March 10, 2015. Retrieved April 2016 (http://www.ancient-origins.net/myths-legends/omens-ancient-world-001435).

Oppenheim, A. Leo. *Ancient Mesopotamia*. Chicago, IL: University of Chicago Press, 1977.

Schomp, Virginia. *Ancient Mesopotamia*. New York, NY: Scholastic, 2004.

"Science and Superstition." The Oriental Institute, 2014. Retrieved April 2016 (https://oi.uchicago.edu/research/symposia/science-and-superstition-interpretation-signs-ancient-world).

Withshire, Katharine. *Ancient Mesopotamia*. New York, NY: Oxford University Press, 2005.

INDEX

ABOUT THE AUTHOR

Laura Loria is a writer and teaching assistant in upstate New York, where she lives with her husband and two children. She holds a bachelor's degree in elementary education with a concentration in history. While in college, she studied Middle Eastern history and developed a passion for learning about cultures around the world. She was inducted into the National History Honor Society, Phi Alpha Theta, during her junior year. Her favorite writing projects are on historical topics because she finds stories from the past to be fascinating.

PHOTO CREDITS

Cover, p. 1 Heritage Images/Hulton Archive/Getty Images; p. 3 Tolga Tezcan/Shutterstock.com; pp. 5, 27, 29, 31, 37 DEA/G. Dagli Orti/De Agostini/Getty Images; p. 7 Culture Club/Hulton Archive/Getty Images; p. 9 Ancient Art & Architecture Collection/© AAAC/Topham/The Image Works; p. 11 Dorling Kindersley/Thinkstock; p. 13 Private Collection/ © Look and Learn/Bridgeman Images; p. 15 © Interphoto/Alamy Stock Photo; pp. 17 Private Collection/Ancient Art and Architecture Collection Ltd./Bridgeman Images; p. 19 Essam Al-Sudani/AFP/Getty Images; p. 21 De Agostini Picture Library/Getty Images; p. 23 Werner Forman/Universal Images Group/Getty Images; p. 25 Louvre, Paris, France/Ancient Art and Architecture Collection Ltd./Bridgeman Images; p. 33 L. De Masi/De Agostini/Getty Images; 35 DEA/A. Dagli Orti/De Agostini/Getty Images; p. 39 Print Collector/Hulton Archive/Getty Images; p. 41 PHAS/Universal Images Group/Getty Images; cover, p. 1 tower of babel graphic Santi0103/Shutterstock.com; back cover and interior pages background map Marzolino/Shutterstock.com; cover and interior pages background textures and patterns zffoto/Shutterstock.com, Elena Larina/Shutterstock.com, Ilaszlo/Shutterstock.com

Designer: Michael Moy; Editor: Heather Moore Niver; Photo Researcher: Heather Moore Niver